LOTS OF THINGS TO KNOW ABOUT WEATHER

Emily Bone

Illustrated by
Katia Gaigalova

Designed by
Katie Webb and Lizzie Knott

With expert advice from Dr. Roger Trend

USBORNE QUICKLINKS

For links to websites where you can watch weather videos and experiments, and find even more facts about weather, go to **usborne.com/Quicklinks** and type in the title of this book.

Please follow the internet safety guidelines at Usborne Quicklinks. Children should be supervised online.

Did you know that the biggest ever hailstone was bigger than an adult's head?

Amazing! But what is a hailstone?

You can check the meaning of that word in the glossary on page 62. And there's an index on pages 63-64 to help you search for a topic.

The sweet smell of rain

Have you ever noticed the pleasant smell after it's rained?
You'll never guess why it happens...

The smell is actually made by tiny things, called bacteria, that live in soil.

When raindrops hit dry soil, the bacteria make bubbles full of a chemical that smells fresh and earthy.

Parfum de rain

The bubbles **pop** and release the smell into the air.

The smell has a name – PETRICHOR. It's so pleasant that lots of perfume makers put it into their scents.

Why it's always windy at the seaside

During the day, the wind blows in **from the sea**.

1. In the sunshine, the land heats up more quickly than the sea.

2. Warm air above the land rises up.

3. This pulls in cooler air from above the sea, which makes a breeze.

In the evening, the wind actually **changes direction**.

1. When the Sun goes down, the sea stays warm but the land starts to cool.

2. Warm air above the sea rises up.

3. Cooler air from the land rushes back to the sea.

So refreshing!

A bit cold if you ask me!

Wow! So the sea can change the weather?

Yes! If the ocean is just a tiny bit warmer, it makes the difference more extreme. This can cause big storms on land, with very strong winds.

The weather moves millions of animals

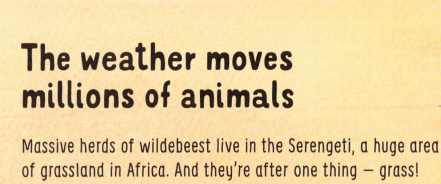

Massive herds of wildebeest live in the Serengeti, a huge area of grassland in Africa. And they're after one thing — grass!

It **rains** in different parts of the Serengeti at different times of the year. At other times it's really dry.

Wildebeest move around the Serengeti, following the rain.

Zebras, gazelles and other animals follow the wildebeest, too.

But WHY are they doing it?

Rain equals new, tasty grass to eat. Plus fresh water to drink, too!

Wind is actually silent

Yes, when you're out on a windy day, it's hard to believe... but the wind **doesn't make a sound!**

It only seems noisy because it's blowing against other things — even your ears.

WHOOSH!

It's really loud!

Yes! The leaves and branches of trees being blown against each other add to the noise too!

WHISTLE!

BONG!

Moonbows

On a rainy day when the sun shines, you might see a **rainbow**. But did you know that when the Sun goes down, there are **moonbows** too?

Ooh, it's pretty! Why do they happen?

A rainbow is caused by the Sun's light hitting water droplets in the sky. At night, the bright Moon shining on mist or rain can do the same thing.

RAINBOW SPOTTER'S GUIDE
Here are some more unusual rainbows:

Fogbow — a white rainbow made in fog or mist

A **second rainbow** or moonbow above the first...

...with the stripes in the opposite order

All moonbows — and rainbows — have stripes in this order: red, orange, yellow, green, blue, indigo, violet.

To see one, you need to have the Moon — or the Sun — behind you.

An **upside-down rainbow** high up in a wispy cloud

A **full circle rainbow**

All rainbows are full circles, but you usually don't see the whole thing unless you're up really high, in a plane or on a mountain.

Reading the clouds

Did you know, you can predict the weather by studying the clouds? Look closely and you'll notice lots of different types of clouds. They all have their own names and mean something different.

Cumulus clouds usually mean bright, sunny weather is coming.

Thin, wispy **cirrus** clouds high up in the sky probably mean changeable weather.

If you see dull **nimbostratus** clouds, you're in for a rainy day.

A thin, white blanket of high **cirrostratus** clouds might mean drizzle, mist or fog.

This huge, dark cloud is a **cumulonimbus**. There's going to be a storm with heavy rain, thunder and lightning.

MONDAY

TUESDAY

WEDNESDAY

THURSDAY

FRIDAY

BOOM!

CRACK!

Some clouds are really **rare**. They only form under special conditions.

Mammatus clouds are very bumpy. They often form just before there's a big storm.

Lenticular clouds look like spaceships or hats. They form because of wind blowing over mountains.

Fallstreak holes are parts of clouds that become frozen and drop down. They're punched out by planes flying through them.

Some clouds even look like waves. They're made by winds blowing at different speeds.

What are clouds, anyway?

They're just a bunch of water droplets all clumped together in the sky. When the water droplets get too heavy, they fall from the clouds as rain.

Winters used to be much, much colder...

Around 500 years ago, in some parts of the world, winters became bitterly cold. Many rivers froze solid for weeks on end. On the icy River Thames in London, exciting fairgrounds were set up on the frozen river, known as **Frost Fairs**.

In 1814, thousands of people came to enjoy the many activities at the last ever Frost Fair – all on top of the thick ice.

Come and get your mince pies here!

Hot chocolate!

Wheee!

Fishermen attached wheels to their boats and gave rides.

Let us take you for the ride of your lives!

Even kings and queens visited the fair.

Your Highnesses!

Oooh!

At this fair, people watched an elephant walking up and down the ice.

Err... he looks heavy?!

Fairs came to an end when the weather warmed up and the ice began to melt. After the last fair, the climate began to change.

Is that a crack?!

Careful!

What made it so much colder?

Sometimes, the Sun goes through phases when it produces less heat. That makes the weather on Earth much cooler, with chilly summers and very harsh winters.

Bugs can tell you the temperature

Did you know you can tell how hot it is outside without a thermometer? All you need is a... **cricket**!

Here's how to do it.
First find a cricket and a timer.
Then, count how many times the cricket **chirps** in eight seconds, and add five.
That's the temperature in degrees Celsius.

So 20 chirps plus 5 equals 25°C!

In degrees Fahrenheit —
count the number of chirps
in 14 seconds, then add 40.

45 chirps plus 40 equals 85°F!

Is it true that crickets make a chirping sound by rubbing the rough edges of their wings together?

Yes! They need the heat of the Sun to give their bodies energy to work properly. The hotter it gets, the quicker they can move their bodies, and the more they chirp!

THE BUG THERMOMETER

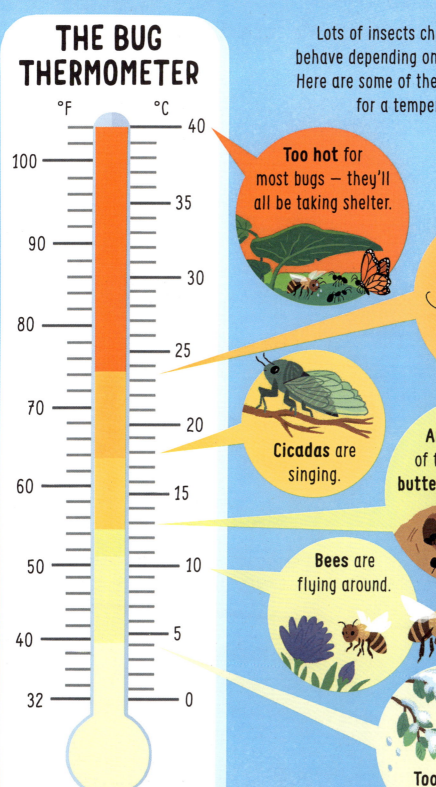

°F °C

100 — — 40

— — 35

90 — — 30

80 — — 25

70 — — 20

60 — — 15

50 — — 10

40 — — 5

32 — — 0

Lots of insects change the way they behave depending on how hot or cold it is. Here are some of the bugs you can rely on for a temperature check:

Too hot for most bugs – they'll all be taking shelter.

Cockroaches are flying around.

Cicadas are singing.

Ants come out of their nests and **butterflies** are flying.

Bees are flying around.

Too cold for most bugs.

The biggest storms have names

Some parts of the world have **hurricanes** — massive storms with extremely violent winds and torrential rain. As soon as one forms, it's given a name.

In some countries, members of the public suggest names and send them to weather scientists.

The group of scientists agree on a list of names for the year, following the letters of the alphabet. It's usually a girl's name, followed by a boy's.

Hurricanes can do a huge amount of damage. Naming them makes it easier for reporters and emergency services to warn people when one's coming.

Hurricanes form at sea and rush towards land. From space, they look like huge, swirling clouds.

The hole in the middle is called the EYE. It's an area of calm weather in the storm.

Storm Ilaria to hit land, September 2nd!

This shows what a hurricane looks like from space.

Hurricanes are also known as cyclones and typhoons.

No rain, guaranteed!

Travel with **No Rain Tours**, and we'll take you on the trip of a lifetime. To the **driest deserts** in the world! But they're not always hot...

Here's where we'll stop:

If you like sand, you'll love the Arabian Desert. Less than 100mm (4in) of rain falls in a whole year!

THE ARABIAN DESERT, ASIA

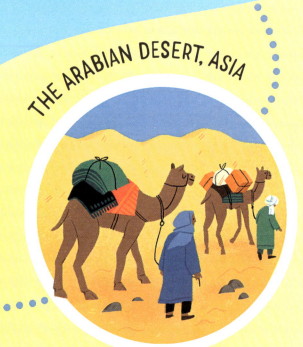

THE MOJAVE DESERT, USA

Next stop, the Mojave Desert, USA. In an area called Death Valley, it can go for an amazing **40 months** with hardly any rain!

This place is scorching. It holds the record for the hottest ever air temperature on Earth, 56.7°C (134°F) – WOW!

THE SAHARA DESERT, AFRICA

Even drier! At our next destination, the Sahara Desert, less than 1mm (0.03in) of rain has fallen in some parts for **hundreds of years**.

THE ATACAMA DESERT, SOUTH AMERICA

Drier still! Areas of this desert haven't had any rain falling for an incredible **500 years** – welcome to the Atacama!

THE MCMURDO DRY VALLEYS, ANTARCTICA

Our final stop is also our driest – by far! The McMurdo Dry Valleys in Antarctica haven't had any rain for **two million years**.

Make sure you pack your hat and scarf, and a bottle of water. It never gets any warmer than -14°C (6.8°F) – BRRR!

Snow can make its own snowballs

Have you ever made a big snowball? You start with a little clump of snow, then roll it along to make it bigger and bigger. With a little help from the wind, snow can do the same thing... **to itself**!

It happens on flat ground, when strong winds blow wet, sticky snow into balls. These balls are called **snow rollers**.

Trails behind the balls show how far they've rolled.

Why haven't I seen these before?

They're really rare! The snow has to be exactly the right amount of sticky. And the wind must be strong, but not too strong as it would blow the ball apart.

Ice can grow hair

Ice isn't just the slippery stuff you see on windows and roads. Ice combined with a particular type of fungus can make an amazing pattern known as **hair ice**.

Exidiopsis effusa is a type of fungus — a plant-like living thing — that grows on rotting wood.

When it gets really cold, water in the wood usually freezes. But the fungus stops this from happening normally.

> You will NOT freeze, water!

Instead, it forces the water out into the cold air, where it immediately freezes into super thin strands of ice. These look like **white hair**.

> If it stays cold enough, hair ice can last for days.

> Ooh, look at my new hairdo!

21

The fastest winds on Earth can be three times faster than a speeding car

These winds are inside violent, whirling wind storms called **tornadoes**, that reach down to the ground from huge, black storm clouds.

The tornadoes with the strongest winds are so fierce that they rip off roofs...

...and flip over big trucks.

Once, a tornado picked up a whole house and carried it almost 100m (320ft) – the length of a football field!

Hailstones (balls of ice) the size of tennis balls come out of tornadoes too. YIKES!

If a tornado reaches a lake or river, it sucks out the water...

...and its fish too!

It's raining fish!

Help! Where do tornadoes happen?

Most are in America, in an area known as Tornado Alley. Read about them here!

Over a thousand tornadoes happen in Tornado Alley every year.

The fastest ever winds inside a tornado were an incredible 480km (300 miles) per hour. They happened in Bridge Creek, Oklahoma, on May 3rd, 1999.

Also know as **twisters**, they're most likely in spring, from March to June.

Tornadoes don't just come from storm clouds. **Fire tornadoes** can form in ferocious wildfires.

And when it's really hot and dry, there can be small tornadoes of sand or dust, called **dust devils**.

Snowflakes can be plates...

...or **needles**, or grow **branches**. In fact, snowflakes come in all kinds of surprising shapes.

Snowflakes begin to form when water droplets inside clouds freeze into tiny ice crystals. **Very cold** clouds make fairly **simple** snowflake shapes.

NEEDLE

TRIANGLE

ROSETTE

PLATE

STAR

No two snowflakes are EXACTLY the same shape. This is because we all melt slightly, in different ways, after we've formed.

There are more water droplets in warmer clouds. These freeze onto snowflakes and gradually make them grow.

A **warmer** cloud makes more **complex**, prettier snowflake shapes, with six clear arms each.

There are so many different shapes!

Yes! These snowflakes are known as DENDRITES, which means tree-like. They're plates that have grown BRANCHES.

One storm has been raging for over 300 years...

...but you won't see it unless you have a really big telescope. Because it's on **another planet**!

There's a massive storm on **Jupiter** that's so big it could swallow the whole of Earth. It's called the **Great Red Spot**.

It's made of wide swirling clouds, like a hurricane. Winds in the storm can reach an incredible 650km (400 miles) per hour.

Why is it red?

Chemicals and gases in the cloud make it red! In fact, different clouds and storms are what gives Jupiter all those stripes.

Interplanetary forecast

On **Neptune**,
it's really rainy.
But instead of water
it rains... diamonds!

WHOOSH!

WAHEY!

WEEE!

Watch out for dust storms
on **Mars**. These can cover
the entire planet.

It's going to be a scorcher on **Venus**.
Temperatures here can reach 480°C
(900°F) — hot enough to melt metal.

On Jupiter's moon,
Europa, it's really cold.
The whole moon is covered
in a thick sheet of ice.

City weather

Compared to the countryside, the weather in cities is...

A lot **windier**! Any wind is forced between buildings and down narrow streets, making it feel stronger.

Warmer! All the buildings and roads absorb heat, and this warms up the air around them.

Rainier! A mixture of hotter air, dust and fumes creates more clouds. This makes it rain more.

Oof, it's a scorcher!

Shorts or umbrella?

Both!

How trees make it rain

Rainforests are big, hot, tropical forests, packed full of trees. They're also extremely rainy. Here's why...

1. Tall rainforest trees have big, wide leaves. When it rains, they catch a lot of the water.

4. The heat makes the damp air rise up. As it cools it turns into rain clouds.

2. Sunshine heats up the water on the leaves.

CRAWK!

3. The water mixes with the air, making it very damp and steamy.

Lots of rainforest plants live high up, clinging to the trees. The air is so wet, their roots dangle in the air and drink the water.

29

Fire weather

In some parts of the world, it doesn't rain for months and the ground dries out completely. If it's windy too, this leads to one thing — **wildfires**.

Dry plants catch fire very easily. Lots of things can start fires:

Sparks from **machinery**

Campfires not put out properly

Sun shining through **broken glass**

Lightning striking the dry ground often starts fires too.

Strong winds make fires more ferocious and help them to spread.

Big wildfires are very dangerous. They can burn out of control and cause a huge amount of damage.

Helicopters and small planes have to drop water to put out the flames.

But smaller fires keep areas healthy. Some plants even rely on them to grow.

Fires burn old plants, leaving space for new ones.

The hard seed pods on eucalyptus trees only open and scatter their seeds in the heat.

POW!

The ash left behind after a fire feeds the soil, too.

Rain food

In April, in parts of China, India and southeast Asia, strong winds bring a dramatic change in the weather, with six months of very heavy rain. This is the **monsoon season**.

Some of the crops in this region depend on the rain.

Tea bushes start to grow fresh and juicy new leaves. These are picked and turned into **tea**.

Tea of the season

After I pick the leaves, they're dried.

Rainy Day Cuppa

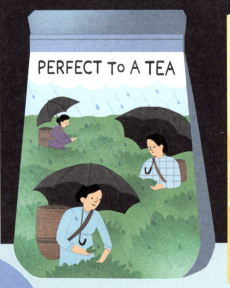

PERFECT TO A TEA

Tea picked at the start of the rainy season is extra strong. It's called Monsoon Tea.

Monsoon Blend

Rice comes from plants that can only grow in fields flooded by heavy rain.

DOWNPOUR RICE

The rice is ready to be harvested when the monsoon season ends.

Wherever it rains a lot, grass grows green and juicy.
Eating lots of grass helps cows to make lots of tasty, creamy **milk**.

In fact, India produces the most milk in the world!

Green Grass Milk

Misty Milk Yogurt

The milk is made into **yogurt** and **cheese**.

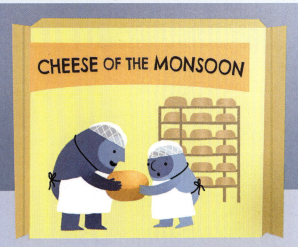

CHEESE OF THE MONSOON

Why the sky is blue on sunny days

Sunlight isn't just the **white-yellow** light we see during the day. It's made up of **blues, reds, oranges, greens** and **purples**, too.

When sunlight reaches the Earth's air, the blue part of the light is scattered (sent in different directions) across the sky. This makes the sky look blue.

Wow, what a bright blue sky!

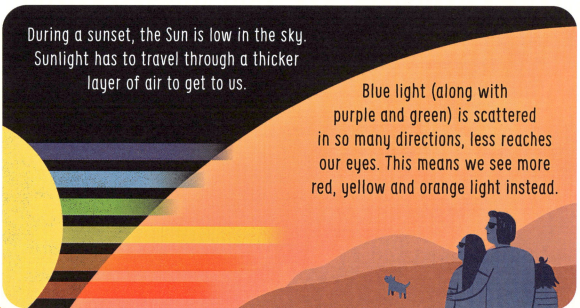

During a sunset, the Sun is low in the sky. Sunlight has to travel through a thicker layer of air to get to us.

Blue light (along with purple and green) is scattered in so many directions, less reaches our eyes. This means we see more red, yellow and orange light instead.

Sunsets are brighter after it's rained

Rain washes away lots of the dust and pollution in the air, leaving it clean and clear. This makes the sunset look especially vivid and spectacular.

Clouds reflect sunlight back down to the ground too, adding to the effect.

Why don't we see a beautiful sunset every night?

Because the sky needs to be slightly cloudy and damp, and fairly clean for us to see a sunset like this.

The place where it rained non-stop for a year

Well almost! Maunawili on the island of Oahu, Hawaii, USA, holds the record for the longest **non-stop rain** – **331 days** in total in 1939-1940.

Hawaii is a collection of islands in the Pacific Ocean. If you live there, you've got to **love** rain because it rains. A lot. Here's why...

1. Warm, damp air is blown in from the sea and up the mountains.

2. As it rises, tiny droplets of water in the air cool down...

3. ...and turn into big rain clouds.

Better take my umbrella – again!

Don't worry, I'm sure it'll stop. Or will it?

It's so wet in Hawaii, that there are over **two hundred words** for different types of rain in the Hawaiian language. Here are just a few:

Ililani
Rain when you weren't expecting it.

I'm NOT dressed for this!

Kili noe
Soft misty rain that cools you off on a hot day.

Ahhhh, that's better!

Why does it always rain on ME?

Kuāu
Rain without wind over a small area.

Hukihe'enehu
Rain that means it's a good time to go fishing.

Come on, we're going to get a good haul!

When rain falls, it can be... red!

Sometimes, there's more than just rain inside a cloud. Sand from the Sahara Desert in Africa can blow thousands of miles before raining down over northern Europe.

The baking hot Sahara Desert is covered with fine sand and dust. Strong winds blow the dust into a huge cloud, up high into the sky.

The cloud is blown a long way by the wind. As it passes over different countries, it turns the sky a hazy yellow.

MORE STRANGE SHADES OF WEATHER...

In parts of the Arctic and Antarctic, snow can turn **pink**.

This is because pink, plant-like creatures called **algae** grow on the snow.

Eventually, it collides with thick rain clouds over Europe. The dust mixes with water droplets...

...and falls to the ground as **red rain**.

Everything is getting covered in a layer of orange-red dust!

I can't see! What's going on?

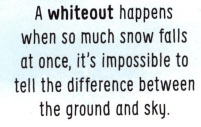

A **whiteout** happens when so much snow falls at once, it's impossible to tell the difference between the ground and sky.

The hottest thing on Earth

Lightning is five times hotter than the surface of the Sun. But it's actually caused by ice!

Inside a huge storm cloud, there are lots of balls of ice – hail – swirling around, along with droplets of **rain** and **snow**.

As the hail, rain and snow bump and rub against each other, they create sparks of electricity...

Oof!

Ouch!

Sorry!

Spark!

Flash!

Excuse me!

Pickles can melt snow

When the weather's very cold or snowy, it's important to keep roads ice-free and safe.

Usually, big trucks drop **salt** on the roads.

Salt makes it harder for water to freeze!

But the salty water runs into rivers, and it can kill the animals that live there.

Now, cities are using different ways to melt snow instead. This includes...

...the liquid left behind from **cheese making**.

...beet juice.

...the liquid leftover from jars of **pickles**.

They can be a bit smelly, but they're much less harmful!

The warmer the weather, the bigger the spiders

Did you know that a long spell of warm weather at the end of summer can lead to **bigger spiders**?

Spiders eat all kinds of bugs. As long as the weather is warm, bugs stay alive.

YUM! More bugs means there's more for me to eat, and I get bigger!

Spiders and the bugs they eat can't survive when it gets too cold.

I don't think I want bigger spiders?

Don't worry, even the bigger ones are more scared of you and will probably try to stay out of your way!

43

Will it rain tomorrow?

Different instruments are used to measure all kinds of things about the weather. Their readings are fed into a massive **weather supercomputer**, and it does lots of calculations to give us our weather forecasts.

ANEMOMETER

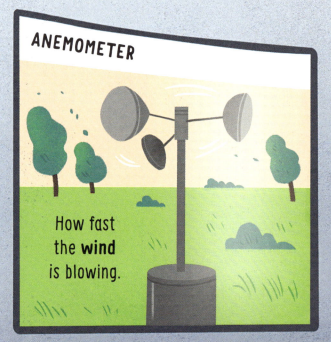

How fast the **wind** is blowing.

HYGROMETER

How much **water** is in the air.

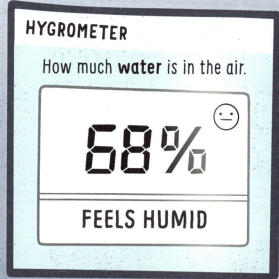

68%

FEELS HUMID

THERMOMETER

Air **temperature**.

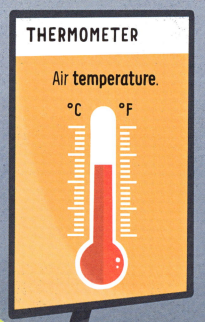

°C   °F

WEATHER SATELLITE

Flies above the Earth, measuring the temperature and thickness of **clouds**.

RAIN GAUGE

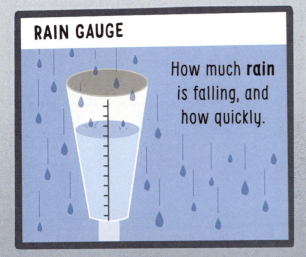

How much **rain** is falling, and how quickly.

WEATHER STATION

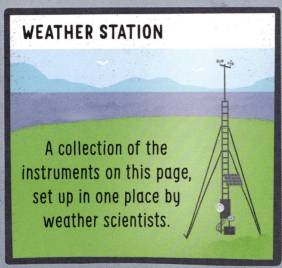

A collection of the instruments on this page, set up in one place by weather scientists.

BAROMETER

Measures **air pressure** — the weight of air pushing down around you.

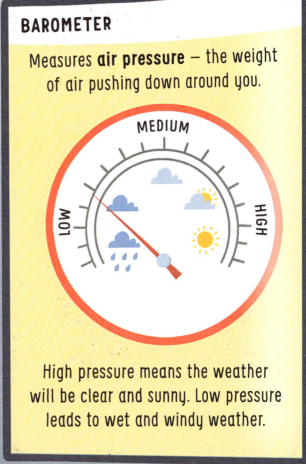

LOW   MEDIUM   HIGH

High pressure means the weather will be clear and sunny. Low pressure leads to wet and windy weather.

See, it WILL rain tomorrow! But you don't ALWAYS need instruments to measure the weather... Turn the page to find out how!

Measuring wind

There's a way of measuring how fast the wind is blowing, just by looking around you. It's called the **Beaufort Scale**, and it goes from 0-12.

LEVEL 2 LIGHT BREEZE

rustle

rustle

6-11KM (4-7 MILES) PER HOUR

Leaves rustle and you can feel the wind on your face.

LEVEL 6 STRONG BREEZE

39-49KM (25-31 MILES) PER HOUR

Umbrellas turn inside out, large branches move and there are big waves at sea.

LEVEL 5 FRESH BREEZE

29-39KM (19-24 MILES) PER HOUR

Small trees sway and leaves are blown from the branches.

0   1   2   3   4   5   6

Weather doesn't just come from the sky...

When volcanoes erupt, they can make weather too — flashing lightning, crashing thunder and heavy rain. The very biggest eruptions can even change the weather all around the world...

Some volcanoes shoot thick clouds full of ash and rock high up into the sky.

WHOOSH!

These make little sparks, which jump out in all directions as... lightning!

CRACK!

There's thunder too.

BOOOOM!

Sometimes, ash clouds mix with clouds already in the sky, making heavy, gloopy rain.

YUCK!

On the evening of April 5th, 1815, Mount Tambora in Indonesia erupted. It was the biggest volcanic eruption ever recorded, and it spewed out clouds full of ash for four months.

BOOM!

The thick clouds blocked out the Sun. In Indonesia, the weather cooled. Crops began to die and people starved.

The cloud whooshed high up into the sky and blew around the world.

WHOOSH!

What's happened to my peach trees?

As far away as Europe and North America, summer never arrived that year. It snowed in July and harvests failed.

I can feel the warm Sun again – woo hoo!

Temperatures stayed low for three years, and it was hard for people to grow any food. Finally, by 1818, all the ash had fallen out of the sky and summer returned.

Weather gods

Long, long ago, before people understood why weather happened, many believed that it was down to their **gods** and **godesses**.

I'm really FURIOUS!

Zeus was the ancient **Greek** god of weather. If he was angry with someone, he threw lightning bolts at them.

The **Aztecs**, who lived in parts of Mexico, thought their god **Tlaloc** ruled over the rain. He had the power to water crops and make them grow... or not.

Boom! Thunder!

Norse people of northern Europe believed that thunder was the sound of the god **Thor** riding into battle.

Err, I think I'll let it rain today!

CRACK!

In **Finland**, people believed the god **Ukko** made the sound of thunder by driving his chariot through the skies.

BOOM!

For the Yoruba people of western Africa, **Oya** was goddess of the winds. She had the power to make trees dance, birds fly and clouds move. She also helped plants to grow.

PFFFFFF!

Yu Shi, the ancient **Chinese** god of rain, carried a jug full of water. When this water splashed out, rain fell from the sky.

Oops!

Groundhogs can predict the weather...

...or can they? People have always looked for signs in nature that might help them predict the weather. But these are not always reliable...

Guess which of the following are TRUE or FALSE. Answers on the next page...

1 A red sunset means the weather will most likely be dry and sunny the next day.

2 The cows are lying down! It'll rain later!

3 Flowers keep their petals open if the weather is going to be sunny, and close them if it's going to rain.

Ooh, better get inside, quick!

4 The number of fogs in August equals the number of snows in December.

5 If the Moon is clearly visible and not covered by clouds, there will be a frost.

Clear Moon, frost soon!

6 February 2nd in America is known as **Groundhog Day**. A groundhog is like a big squirrel. One groundhog is chosen and named **Punxsutawney Phil**. If he sees his shadow, there will be six more weeks of wintry weather.

If I don't cast a shadow, winter will end soon!

ANSWERS

1. TRUE! Red sunsets happen when tiny specks of dust are trapped in the air, turning the sky red. Dust is usually only trapped when the air is calm and warm – meaning the next day will have good weather.

2. FALSE! Cows lie down because they need a rest.

3. TRUE! Some flowers close their petals before it rains. This could be to protect them from being damaged.

4. FALSE! There's no reason why fog – a cloud that forms because of cool, damp air close to the ground – would have any relation to it snowing later in the year.

5. TRUE – well kind of... Clouds act like a blanket, trapping heat in the air. In winter, a clear night sky usually means it's colder, so there will probably be a frost in the morning.

6. FALSE! Phil has only been right 39% of the time since he started predicting the weather 120 years ago.

Hailstones are getting bigger...

...and it's because the world is getting **warmer**.

Hailstones form inside huge storm clouds, when small drops of water freeze into ice.

As they're blown up and down, more water freezes onto the hailstones, making them **BIGGER**...

...and **BIGGER**...

...until they finally get so heavy they fall out of the cloud and to the ground.

Many cars and factories pump out harmful gases that trap heat in the air, making the planet warmer. This is known as **climate change**.

Warmer air makes bigger, wetter storm clouds with stronger winds. The strong winds keep hailstones blowing around for longer...

...leading to **GIANT** balls of hail.

How big is giant?

A giant hailstone is bigger than a tennis ball - yikes!

55

The Sun has storms too

The **Sun** is a massive ball of very hot burning gases, that are constantly churning and exploding. Sometimes there are especially huge explosions. This is a **solar storm**.

When there is a **solar storm**, it sends a stream of rays hurtling through space.

Whoosh!

Booom!

I'm really, really far away from Earth. But my explosions give Earth all its light and heat!

Some deserts are wet

Deserts are dry, right? Not always... For part of the year, some deserts get **a lot** of rain. And when they do, something extraordinary happens.

This is the Sonoran Desert in North America. It's the end of June, and it has hardly rained at all since January. This is all about to change...

From July to September, sudden, torrential downpours flood the ground with water, and fill up dry river valleys.

Cactus plants swell up, storing the newly-fallen rain.

Flowers spring up from the ground and bloom on plants.

Insects visit the flowers.

Desert birds lay eggs, as they know there will be enough food for their babies.

Spadefoot toads flock to pools to lay eggs.

Big **lizards**, called gila monsters, come out to drink and eat.

59

Weather records

Wow! On display here you can see the most extreme, **record-breaking** weather of all time!

RAINIEST PLACE

Mawsynram, India, gets an incredible 11.8m (38ft) of rain every year. That's higher than a house!

It really is SCORCHING!

SUNNIEST PLACE

Yuma in Arizona, USA, has up to 13 hours of sunshine every day.

HOTTEST PLACE

Ground temperatures reach 70.7°C (159.3°F) in the **Lut Desert** in Iran.

SNOWIEST PLACE

Aomori City, Japan, has an astounding 8m (26ft) of snow fall each winter.

COLDEST PLACE

Antarctica! Get your coats, because temperatures on the **Eastern Antarctic Plateau** can drop to a very chilly –94°C (–137.2°F) below freezing.

WINDIEST PLACE

It's super windy in Antarctica. In **Commonwealth Bay**, you can regularly expect winds of 240km (150 miles) an hour.

The world's weather is quickly becoming more extreme. So it's likely that all of the records here will be broken in the future.

Glossary

Here you can find out what some of the words in this book **mean**...

air pressure – the weight of air pushing down on you. How high or low the pressure is affects what the weather will be like.

Beaufort Scale – a scale used to measure how fast the wind is blowing, just by looking outside.

climate change – a gradual, long-term change in Earth's weather – usually more rain and higher temperatures – caused by the warming of the planet.

cumulonimbus – a tall, dark **storm** cloud that can produce heavy rain, **hailstones**, **lightning** and **thunder**.

desert – a very dry area where very little rain falls.

fog – thick cloud low to the ground.

hailstone – a ball of ice that forms when water freezes inside a **storm** cloud.

hurricane – a massive, very violent **storm** with extremely fast winds that forms at sea and moves onto land.

lightning – very hot sparks of electricity that leap out of clouds during a **storm**.

monsoon season – months of very heavy rain that happen in some parts of the world.

moonbow – a **rainbow** at night, caused by bright moonlight reflecting off raindrops.

petrichor – the smell made after rain hits dry ground.

rainbow – a bright arc in the sky caused by sunlight reflecting off raindrops.

rainforest – a thick forest with hot, rainy weather all year round.

thunder – the sound of **lightning** heating up the air around it.

tornado – a violent, spinning wind **storm** that reaches down to the ground from some **storm** clouds.

snowflake – tiny ice crystals that join together inside a cloud before falling to the ground.

solar storm – a **storm** on the Sun, caused by explosions of gas.

storm – a period of disturbed weather with strong winds. There is often heavy rain, **hailstones** and **thunder** and **lightning**, too.

whiteout – heavy snow and strong winds that make the sky turn white.

wildfire – a fire in grassland or forest that burns over a big area.

Index

Series editor: Ruth Brocklehurst
Series designer: Stephen Moncrieff

First published in 2023 by Usborne Publishing Ltd., 83-85 Saffron Hill, London EC1N 8RT, United Kingdom. usborne.com Copyright © 2023 Usborne Publishing Limited. The name Usborne and the Balloon logo are registered trade marks of Usborne Publishing Limited. All rights reserved. No part of this publication may be reproduced, stored in a retrieval system, or transmitted in any form or by any means without the prior permission of the publisher. First published in America 2023. UE.